PLANTS Up Close

PLANTS Up Close

JOAN ELMA RAHN

Illustrated with photographs

Houghton Mifflin Company   Boston 1981

Library of Congress Cataloging in Publication Data

Rahn, Joan Elma, 1929–
    Plants up close.
    Summary: Examines five different plants in order to show how the parts of a plant function and how they contribute to the plant's life.
    1. Plants—Juvenile literature.   2. Botany—Morphology—Juvenile literature.   [1. Plants.   2. Botany]
I. Title.
    QK49.R33   582'.04   81-6656
    ISBN 0-395-31677-4   AACR2

Contents

Introduction

What do you see when you see a plant? Stems? Leaves? Perhaps some flowers or fruits? That is all many people notice as they pass a tree or a flower garden. They look quickly but not closely. If you examine a plant carefully, you will find that its parts consist of smaller parts — some of them beautiful, some of them interesting, and many of them both. Furthermore, if you take the time to think about what you see, you will begin to understand how the plant "works" — that is, how its different parts function and how they contribute to the plant's life.

When should you do this? Any day. Begin today, if you like. Of course, probably many more plants attract your attention in summer than in winter, but even the leafless trees of winter can be interesting.

In this book we will look at five different

plants. We begin on a spring day, studying the flower parts of tulips in full bloom.

Then, early in summer, we look at a sugar maple tree and learn something about a tree's leaves — and also a little about its fruits, which have begun to form.

We spend two midsummer days with butternut squash and sunflower; both have two types of flower on the same plant.

On a late summer day we visit rose of Sharon — mostly to watch bumblebees pollinating the flowers and to see how well suited bumblebees and rose of Sharon flowers are to each other.

Finally, we return to the sugar maple tree on a winter day to learn about its growth by looking at its buds and the scars left by fallen bud scales and leaves.

Wherever you live are many other plants, and any day of the year you can learn something from them.

PLANTS Up Close

1 A Spring Day
TULIP

This is a bed of tulip plants. All the tulips of one variety usually bloom at about the same time in spring. Each plant here has an open flower or a flower bud that is just about to open.

A tulip usually has only one long stem with one flower at the top of the stem — which is why we often plant them in groups instead of singly.

Each tulip flower has six tepals; they are the parts most people call petals. There are three outer tepals and three inner tepals. Tepals are usually the same size and color and nearly the same shape, but if you look closely, sometimes you can find a few small differences. In this tulip flower, for example, the outer tepals have pointed tips and the inner ones are rounded.

outer tepal

inner tepal

Here, three tepals have been removed to show the inner parts of the flower.

In the center is the pistil, which is the female part of the flower. It appears white in the photograph. A tulip pistil consists of two parts: the ovary and the stigma.

The ovary is the part of the flower that bears the seeds. At the top of the ovary is the stigma, with three lobes, of which you can see two here. The stigma is the part that receives pollen. If the stigma is not pollinated, no seeds will form in the ovary.

Around the pistil is a ring of stamens, which are the male part of the flower. Each stamen has two parts: a filament and an anther. The filament is the stalk that holds the anther, and the anther produces pollen.

This is a newly opened flower, and you can see a long slit in two of the anthers. The slits will widen, and pollen will be released.

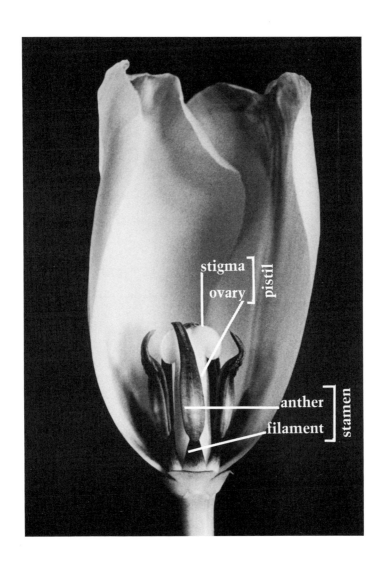

stigma ⎤
         ⎬ pistil
ovary   ⎦

anther ⎤
         ⎬ stamen
filament ⎦

These anthers have opened and have almost turned inside out, revealing their thousands of pollen grains. Each pollen grain appears as a small dot.

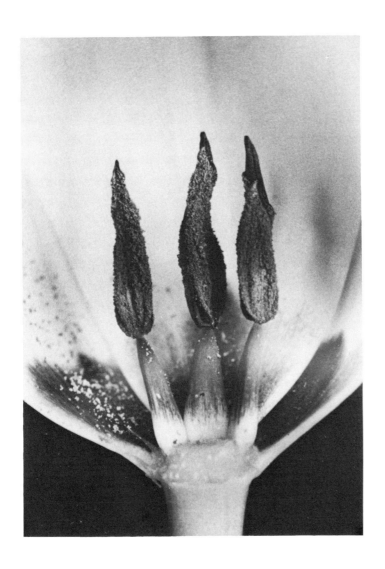

If an insect touches an opened anther, some of the pollen grains will stick to its body. Later, if the insect brushes against a stigma, pollen may rub off, as shown here.

Many small hairs cover the stigma and help to hold any pollen grains that reach them. Once caught among the hairs, pollen is not likely to fall off.

If you cut across a part of a plant, the cut surface is a cross section. The cross section of a tulip ovary, shown here, is nearly triangular in shape. The three corners correspond to the three lobes of the stigma.

In this cross section you see six ovules. These will develop into seeds if the stigma is pollinated.

Actually, a tulip ovary contains more than six ovules. You could make many more cross sections of an ovary — something like slicing a loaf of bread. Each slice across the ovary would have its own ovules.

The six small white spots near the outer edge of the ovary are veins. They carry food, minerals, and water to the ovules as they ripen into seeds.

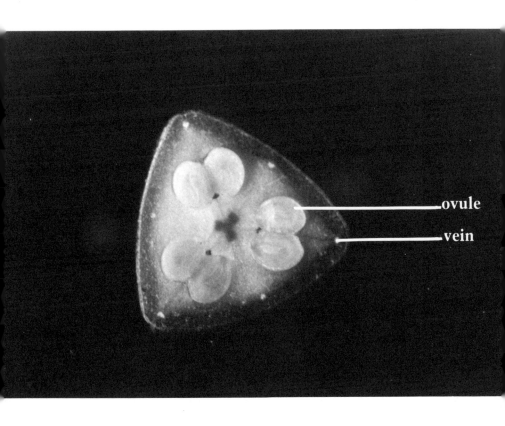

ovule

vein

2 An Early Summer Day

SUGAR MAPLE

This is a sugar maple tree. It has new leaves, only a few weeks old.

You can see two main parts of the tree: the trunk and the crown. The trunk is the thick, woody main stem of the tree. The crown is the leafy portion; it's everything above the ground except the bare lower part of the trunk.

From a distance the crown has a solid appearance. It looks as if it were filled with leaves from side to side, from front to back, and from top to bottom. But this is not so; it just looks that way here.

crown

trunk

If you stand near the tree trunk and look up along it, you see that the crown is "hollow," at least as far as leaves are concerned. The trunk continues up through the crown, but the trunk bears no leaves. Large branches grow from it, and the branches have branches, and so on. The only parts of the tree with leaves are the youngest twigs, at the ends of the branches.

The leaves of the tree manufacture the food that the tree needs to stay alive, and to produce food they must receive sunshine. At the outer edge of the crown, the leaves get sunshine. Any leaves inside the crown — and there are very few — get very little sunshine. It would be wasteful for the tree to form many leaves there.

This photograph shows the upper surface of a sugar maple leaf. We notice two parts: a flat part, called the blade, and a stalk, or petiole. When the leaf was on the tree, it was attached by the petiole.

Inside the petiole are veins that carry water and minerals to the blade. These veins branch out from the top of the petiole and run across the blade.

blade

vein

petiole

This is part of the lower surface of a sugar maple leaf. The major veins stand out from the lower surface more than they do from the upper surface. These veins are strong, and one of their functions is supporting the rest of the blade.

The major veins branch into smaller and smaller veins.

The smallest veins meet and form a network. The dark areas among these veins are the green parts of the leaf. When light shines on them, these green parts manufacture food.

The leaf uses whatever food it needs, and the rest enters the small veins. Here it travels to larger and larger veins, then down the petiole, into the branch, and from there to larger and larger branches. If other parts of the plant need it, the food travels there. Otherwise, it goes down the trunk and finally reaches the root, where it is stored until next spring. Then the food will move back up within the tree to the buds, where new stems and new leaves are about to grow.

Maple leaves grow in pairs along a stem. The two members of a pair are on opposite sides of the stem.

If the stem grows straight up and is not crowded by other stems or leaves, the petioles extend away from it and hold the blades as far out as possible. This puts all the leaf blades in sunlight.

Most of the branches of a sugar maple do not grow straight up. Many grow horizontally, and some of the lower ones even bend down a bit. Most branches are shaded, at least in part, by other branches. In these cases, the petioles bend. Some grow almost parallel with the stem; some bend away from it. How they grow depends on where shade and sunshine are. Each petiole bends away from shade and toward light; this puts the blade in the brightest sunshine possible.

Petioles bend most when they are young and still growing — in spring and early summer. Later in summer, when they have stopped growing, they do not bend or do so very slowly, but by this time each blade is in the best position it can reach.

By putting the blades in sunshine, the bending of the petioles forms a leaf mosaic. As you look down on a leaf mosaic, you see that smaller leaves fit in the spaces among larger leaves. This is why from a distance the crown has such a solid appearance.

This maple tree flowered about a month ago. The flowers have fallen — all but the ovaries, that is. The ovaries have grown into winged fruits, each fruit with two distinct halves, each half with a wing.

At this time of year the fruits are still green.

If you open one half of a maple fruit you may find a young, developing seed. In some fruits there is a seed in each half. In others, only one half has a seed, and the other is empty.

The seed, like the fruit, is green in summer.

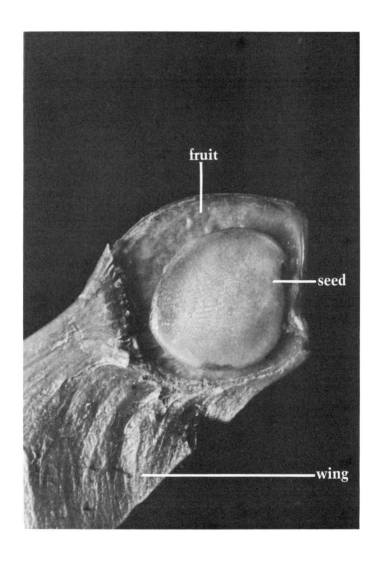

fruit

seed

wing

If you open the green seed carefully, you will find a small, green embryo inside. An embryo is a young plant — in this case, a very young sugar maple tree.

Most of the embryo consists of two cotyledons or seed leaves. These are the first leaves formed by an embryo growing inside a seed. You can see only one of the two cotyledons here because the other one is directly behind it.

The embryo has a root tip, which appears toward the upper right of this photograph. Between the root tip and the cotyledons is a slightly curved stalk called the hypocotyl — which means "below the cotyledons."

The embryo, young as it is, has already grown to be longer than the seed it occupies. It can fit inside the seed only because it has curled. The cotyledons themselves are longer than the seed, and they have begun to fold a little.

The fruits, with their seeds and embryos, will remain on the tree all summer, and the embryos will continue to grow.

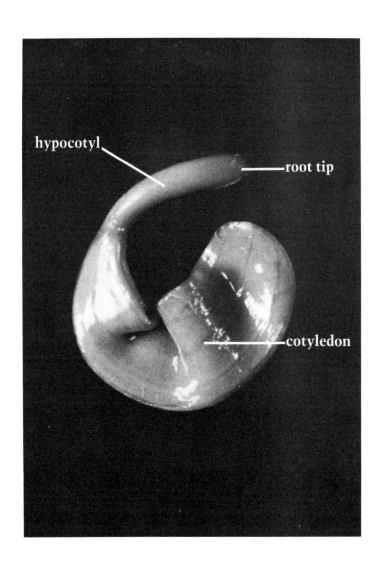

hypocotyl

root tip

cotyledon

3 A Midsummer Day
BUTTERNUT SQUASH

Butternut squash plants are vines, plants with long stems that either trail along the ground or climb on fences or other available supports. The stems are not strong enough to support themselves.

Only a few squash flowers open at a time, and each only lasts a day. However, once flowers begin to appear, new ones open nearly every day until autumn. In midsummer, on the same butternut squash plant, you can find flower buds, open flowers, and fruits at various stages of ripening.

Squash plants cling to their supports by tendrils. When a young tendril first appears, it is coiled in a tight spiral.

This picture includes the same tightly coiled tendril. Below it another one is uncoiling. Each tendril has three branches. One branch of this tendril has uncoiled fully, but the other two branches have barely started to unwind.

We will see the flower bud in this picture again.

A tendril bends slowly back and forth until it touches an object. Then the tip begins to grow around what it has touched.

When the free end of a tendril has grown around a firm support, the tendril coils again, but this time the coil is in the form of a helix. (Many people call a helix a spiral. The "spiral" wire in a "spiral-bound" notebook is really a helix.)

Actually, the tendril has two helices — one coiling in one direction, the other in the opposite direction. This happens because the tendril begins to coil in the middle. As the coiling proceeds from the middle to both ends, the twists are in opposite directions. Many helically coiled tendrils help to support one vine.

A coiled tendril is springy. During a storm, when the vine is battered by strong winds, the coiled tendril stretches, then tightens up again. If it were straight and tight, it probably would break in a high wind.

When tendrils do not find any support, they sometimes shrivel and die. This has happened to the two other branches of the tendril shown here.

Squash has two types of flower: male flowers and female flowers.

Here is a male flower that has been picked and placed on the leaves so that you can see it from the side. It has five large, yellow petals that are joined together in a vaselike shape. In this view you can see only two of the petals. There are also five small, narrow, green sepals, three of which are visible here.

petal

sepal

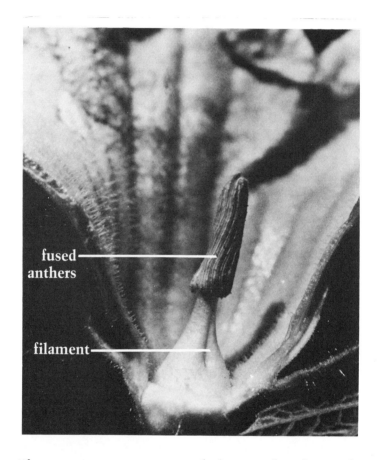

fused
anthers

filament

If you cut away some of the petals of a male squash flower, you will see the stamens in the center. (There is no pistil in a male flower.) There are five stamens, but their anthers are fused together, and so are some of the filaments. Here, five filaments look like two.

In the left photograph, the anthers are just beginning to open; each has two long grooves that will open wider. At right, the anthers have been open for a while, and some pollen grains have emerged.

This is the young bud we saw before. It is a female flower that has not yet opened. In squash, the ovary is located below the petals and sepals; you can see it without looking down into the flower. The ovary will mature into a butternut squash. Already it looks like a tiny squash.

sepal

ovary

When squash plants grow along the ground, female flowers often are partly hidden under the leaves. Therefore, insects usually visit one or more male flowers first. This way, when they enter a female flower, the insects are likely to be carrying pollen.

Three of the five petals have been removed from this female flower. The pistil has three parts: stigmas, style, and ovary.

The three V-shaped stigmas have a velvety surface; their many small hairs pick up pollen grains from visiting insects. The style is the stalk between the ovary and the stigmas. Each pollen grain produces a fine pollen tube that grows inside the style down to the ovary.

What looks like a collar around the style is a nectar gland. The sugary solution it secretes is called nectar. When the flower is open, insects visit it and feed on the nectar. Bees also take it back to their hive.

There are no stamens in a female squash flower.

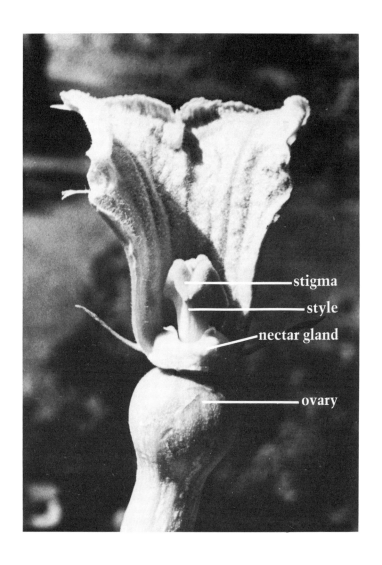

stigma

style

nectar gland

ovary

The sepals, petals, stigmas, style, and nectar gland have fallen from this female flower. All that remains is the ovary, now a young fruit. It will be much larger in autumn, when it ripens.

4 Another Midsummer Day

SUNFLOWER

The common sunflowers raised in gardens usually have one tall, sturdy stem and several large leaves. The lower leaves are spaced far apart on the stem, but near the top they are crowded together. At the top of the stem, among these leaves, is what appears to be a large flower. In fact, the "flower" of a sunflower is really a cluster of many small flowers.

A grouping of several small flowers close together on a plant is called an inflorescence.

Different kinds of plants have different inflorescences. The inflorescence of a sunflower is called a head. The small, individual flowers are called florets. In the upper photograph you are looking down on a sunflower head. The one below shows a head that has been cut in half from top to bottom.

The stem on which a head grows widens at the top and forms a flat surface called a disk. All the florets are on the top of the disk.

A sunflower head has two types of floret: ray florets and disk florets. The ray florets are at the edge of the disk; they have large yellow petals. All the others are disk florets.

The disk florets do not all open at the same time. The outermost ones open first, and the ones in the center of the disk open last.

ray floret

disk floret

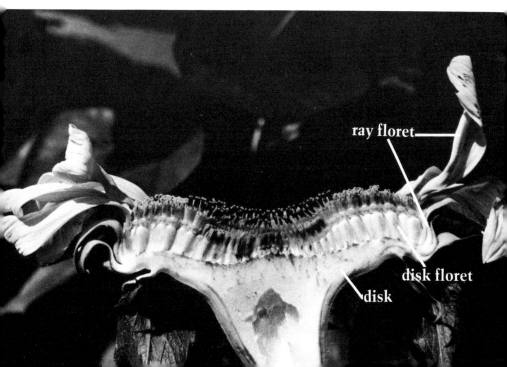

ray floret

disk floret

disk

Here are a few florets taken from a sunflower head. The floret at the left is a ray floret; all the rest are disk florets. The ovaries, like those of squash flowers, appear below all the other flower parts.

Starting at the right and proceeding to the left in this photograph we see —

two very young, unopened disk florets from the center of the head
two slightly older, still unopened disk florets
two open florets with anthers showing
two open florets with stigmas showing
one ray floret

Near the ovary of every sunflower floret still on the disk there is a bract. A bract is a leaflike structure that grows near a flower but is not part of it. One in each pair of disk florets in this photograph has its bract with it. The bracts of all the other florets have been removed.

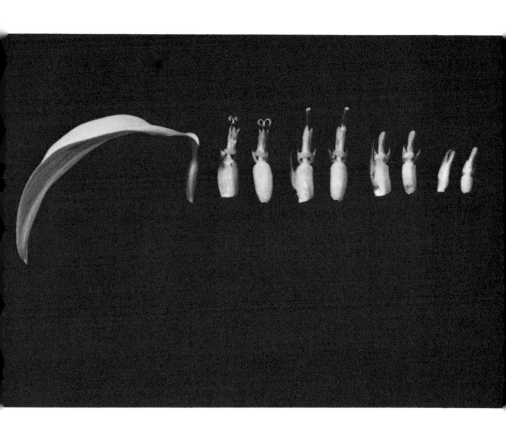

The ovary of each disk floret will ripen into what most people call a sunflower seed. Actually this "seed" is not a seed, but a small fruit called an achene.

The ovary of this floret has been cut open to show you the single ovule inside. When an ovary ripens into an achene, the ovule ripens into the true seed, which some people call a sunflower "meat."

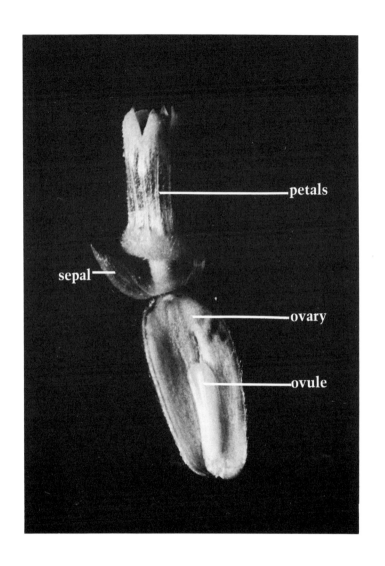

petals

sepal

ovary

ovule

Ray florets also have ovaries, but they never ripen into fruits. The five petals of a ray floret are very long, and they are all joined together and form what looks like one huge petal bent to one side of the floret. Ray florets have the same function that petals do in flowers of many other kinds of plants: they attract pollinating insects.

It is because their petals radiate around the head that ray florets are so named.

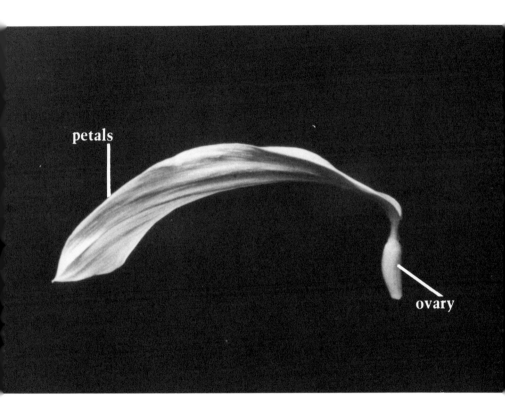

petals

ovary

5 A Late Summer Day

ROSE OF SHARON

Rose of Sharon is a shrub or small tree that blooms during the last half of summer and into autumn. Each flower stays open just one day, but the plant forms new ones daily.

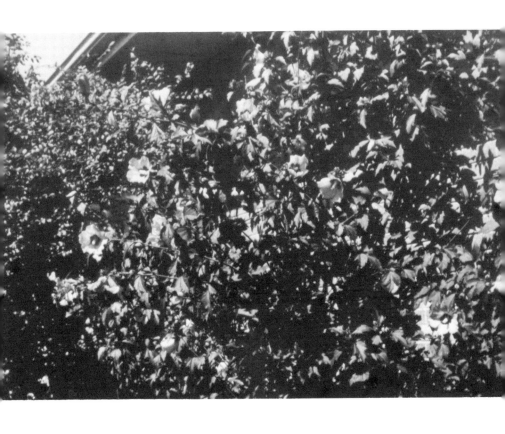

The flowers face outward from the plant. This probably makes them more noticeable to the bumblebees that pollinate them.

Each flower has five petals and five sepals. The petals are large and separate, but the sepals are joined and form a little cup at the base of the flower.

Around the sepals are five small, fingerlike bracts. They are green and look almost like another set of sepals.

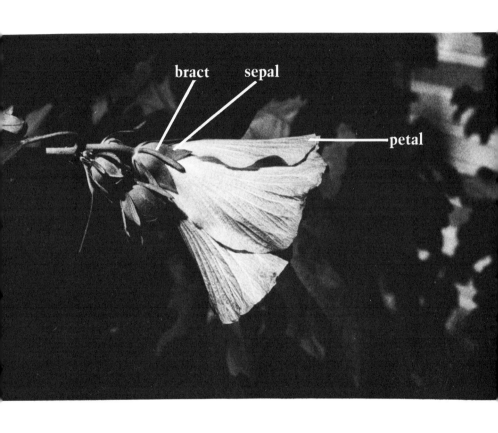

bract sepal petal

This photograph shows the anthers inside a flower bud that is just about to open. The anthers are still closed, but each one has a groove that will open about when the bud opens.

A rose of Sharon flower has many small stamens. Their filaments are all fused into a filament tube that surrounds the pistil and hides most of it.

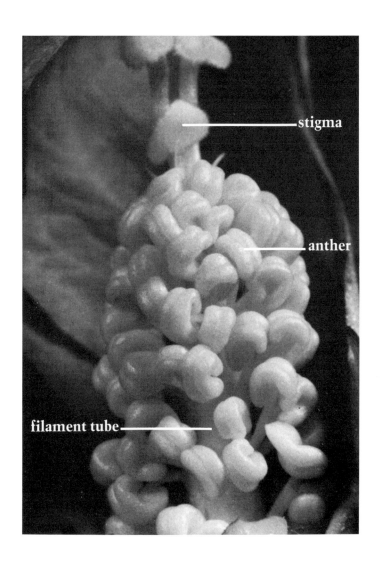

stigma

anther

filament tube

This photograph of the same flower bud shows the stigmas and style extending above the stamens.

The pistil of a rose of Sharon flower has five styles, each with a stigma; four stigmas are visible here. They have a velvety appearance because they are covered by many fine, short hairs.

You can see only the upper ends of some of the styles. The rest is surrounded by the filament tube formed by the stamens.

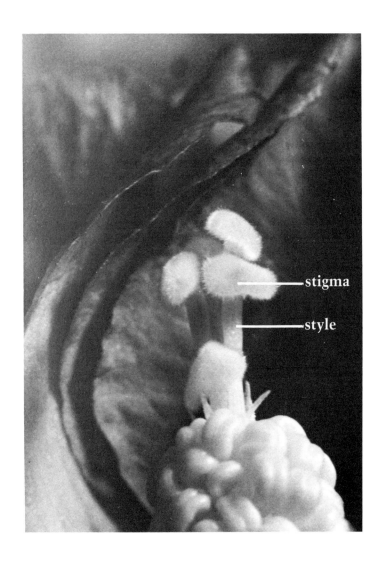

stigma

style

These stamens and pistil of a rose of Sharon flower have been cut down the center to show how the filament tube surrounds the pistil.

Since the flower bud has not yet opened, no insects have visited it, and no pollen grains have reached the stigmas. However, the anthers have opened, and some pollen grains are emerging.

There are several ovules in the ovary.

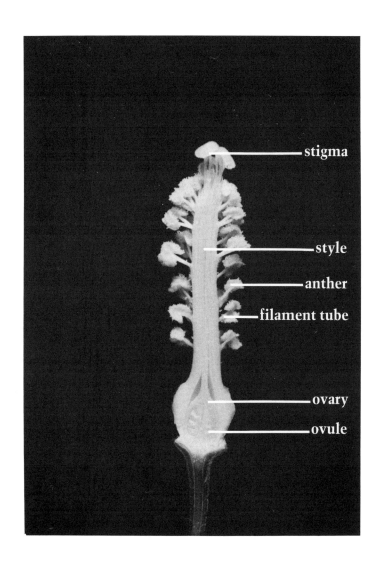

stigma

style

anther

filament tube

ovary

ovule

The pollen grains of insect-pollinated flowers usually are sticky. They cling readily to the bodies of visiting insects and generally remain there even while the insect travels from flower to flower. The pollen grains also cling to each other. As a result, when an insect brushes against the anthers, it is likely to pick up many pollen grains at a time.

This photograph shows a flower that has been open for several hours. So much pollen has emerged that many of the anthers are covered with it. The next insect to visit the flower will probably carry away a large load of pollen.

Notice that a few anthers are still closed. They probably will open before the day is over.

Here a bumblebee, still flying but about to land, brushes a stigma with a foreleg before reaching the stamens. If the bee is carrying pollen from another flower, some will rub off onto the stigma.

Because the flower faces outward, the filament tube extends horizontally. The sturdy tube makes a good platform on which bumblebees can land.

Other insects visit rose of Sharon flowers, but bumblebees are the best pollinators, for they instinctively aim for the filament tube. Smaller insects, like honeybees, often land on the petals and may never touch the stigmas.

Another reason why bumblebees pollinate rose of Sharon flowers so well is that their bodies are large, and they don't have much choice about how to position themselves when they land. Nearly every bumblebee lands with her legs on the anthers and with her abdomen touching the stigmas.

The tip of this bumblebee's abdomen carries pollen grains that she brings from another flower.

After landing, the bumblebee moves about in the flower and gathers more pollen on her body.

By touching the stigmas first and the anthers second, the bumblebee brings about cross-pollination, the pollinating of a stigma with pollen from another flower. Cross-pollination usually produces more seed and healthier seed than self-pollination, whereby a stigma receives pollen from the same flower.

After a bumblebee departs, the stigmas are covered with pollen grains. In many rose of Sharon flowers, the styles, which were straight in the closed buds, curve upward when the flower opens, as shown here, making it even more likely that the bumblebee's abdomen will touch them when she lands.

If you watch a bumblebee moving about in a flower, you will see that she does not move haphazardly. She collects nectar, and her proboscis reaches down between the base of the petals, where the nectar forms.

Although the petals of rose of Sharon flowers are wide and overlap a little, their bases are quite narrow. Between them are small spaces. As you look between the petals, you can just glimpse the sepals. It is the sepals that produce the nectar bees seek.

This rose of Sharon flower is both pink (where it appears grayish in this photo) and red (where it looks black). The red area forms a many-pointed star that the bumblebees can see from a distance. Such a marking in a flower is called a nectar guide. Once an insect learns that a flower with that marking has nectar, similar marks guide it to other flowers on the same kind of plant.

Most of this flower has been removed, but three sepals remain. Each has nectar glands at its base. The glands manufacture nectar and secrete it slowly. When you look between the bases of the petals in an intact flower, it is actually these nectar glands that you see.

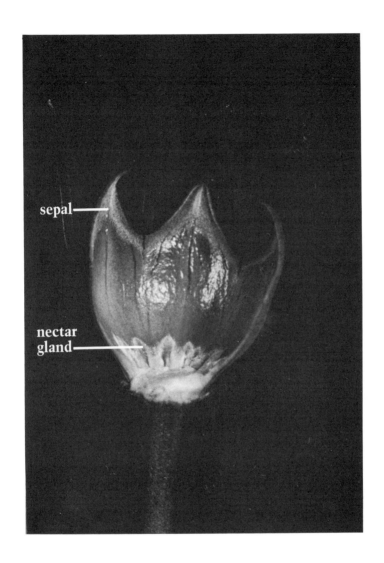

sepal——

nectar
gland——

Here is the cross section of a young fruit from a flower a week or two after pollination. The ovary has enlarged, and the ovules are developing into seeds.

Some of the ovules were cut when the ovary was cut. One was barely grazed by the knife, but in three ovules you can see the embryo sac, the part of the ovule in which the embryo develops. Only one of these embryo sacs was cut at the level at which its young embryo lies.

At this early stage of development, the rose of Sharon embryo is very small and occupies only part of the embryo sac. Eventually it will fill the entire sac.

The embryo sacs here look wet, and they are wet. Each contains liquid tissue called endosperm. The endosperm nourishes the embryo and is used up as it grows.

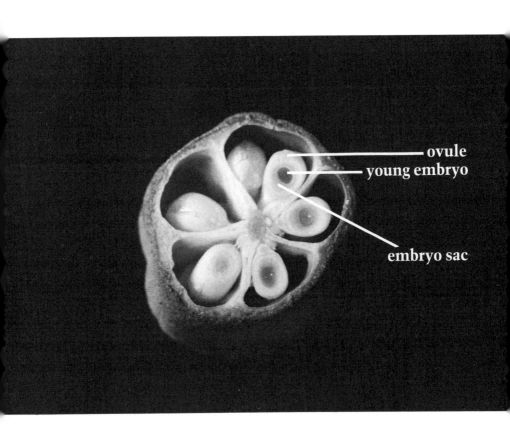

ovule

young embryo

embryo sac

6 A Winter Day

SUGAR MAPLE

It is late winter in this picture. The leaves have fallen from the sugar maple tree a long time earlier, and now, with the branches bare, the tree looks dead. But it is not dead; it is dormant.

A dormant plant is one that is not growing, but dormancy means more than just not growing. Dormant plants often resist extreme environmental conditions. This sugar maple can resist cold weather and the drying effects of winter winds. The tree is almost twenty years old. During its nearly twenty winters it has lived through several nights when the temperature reached at least $-15°F$ (about $-26°C$), and it probably could survive colder temperatures still. It has also lived through many blizzards.

Branches grow in length only at their tips. Every year a branch grows longer during spring and early summer. Then growth slows down and stops in autumn when dormancy sets in. The next year growth starts again in spring.

Each twig in the upper part of the tree and at the edge of the crown was formed last spring and summer. They are last year's growth, the twigs that bore leaves last summer.

The branches from which those twigs grew are older; most are two years old, some are older. As we look farther and farther down on the tree we come to older and older parts.

One of the twigs formed last spring grew to be about eighteen inches in length. Only about the last inch is shown here (magnified 5 times).

Each twig ends in a terminal bud. It is covered with thick leaves called bud scales. You can see five of them this photograph: two with light tips facing each other, one facing you, and two more facing each other.

The other buds on the stem are lateral buds; they grow to the side. During the summer, the lateral buds developed slowly, one just above each leaf. Now that the leaves have fallen, a leaf scar remains where each leaf was attached to the stem. Therefore, each lateral bud is located just above a leaf scar.

Three lateral buds show in this photograph. The one closest to the terminal bud looks almost like one of the bud scales, but there is a very thin leaf scar below it. Each leaf scar of sugar maple reaches about halfway around the stem.

If the terminal bud is healthy, it will open in spring, and the stem that grows from it will increase the length of the branch. If the terminal bud is damaged, and sometimes even if it is not, some of the lateral buds will produce branches.

By the end of its first growing season, each twig is covered with a thin layer of bark.

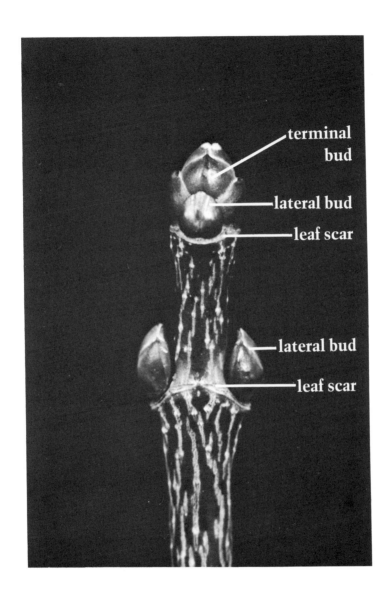

terminal
bud

lateral bud

leaf scar

lateral bud

leaf scar

This photograph shows the lowermost part of last spring's growth and the uppermost part of the growth of the year before. Between them is a ring of bud scale scars. Because bud scales are a type of leaf, when they fall off, they leave their own scars. Like the bud scales themselves, the scars are very close together.

Just below the bud scale scars are two branches. They developed last summer, when two lateral buds opened. Each branch has its own ring of bud scale scars at its base, marking where the bud scales of those buds fell off when they opened.

In sugar maple, each petiole has three veins. They are also called vascular bundles. The leaf scars each contain three bundle scars. These are the scars that formed when the veins broke as the leaf fell from the tree.

The leaf scars of sugar maple do not all have the same shape. Compare this leaf scar with those in the preceding photograph.

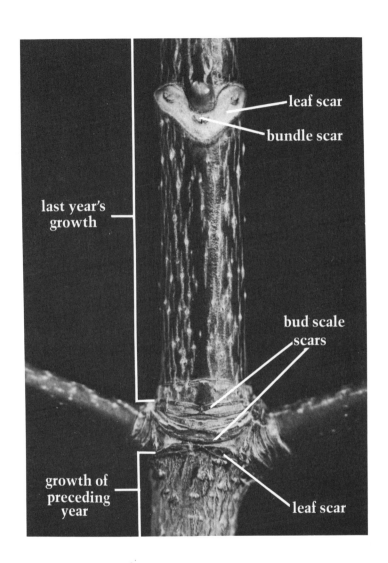

leaf scar

bundle scar

last year's growth

bud scale scars

growth of preceding year

leaf scar

As the stem grows older, it increases in width, and the bark becomes thicker. When this happens, the bark cracks, and so do the leaf scars and the bud scale scars. Lateral buds that remained dormant begin to be covered by the bark.

This is the lower part of the three-year-old growth of the stem and the upper part of the four-year-old growth. A set of bud scale scars separates them.

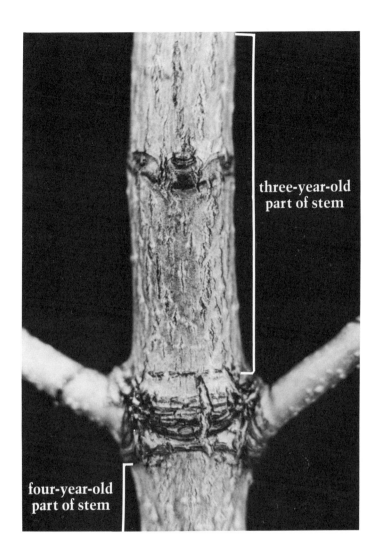

three-year-old part of stem

four-year-old part of stem

The lateral bud and the leaf scar in this five-year-old portion of the stem are becoming less distinct as the bark grows thicker.

None of the stems we are looking at in this chapter will ever bear leaves again. New leaves never form on parts of stems that once had leaves. All of next year's leaves will come from the buds that will open next year.

In older, thicker parts of a sugar maple tree, the leaf scars have become so stretched that they look like dotted lines. The bud scale scars are usually darker and thicker than the leaf scars.

Stems do not grow the same amount each year. How long one grows depends in part on environmental conditions: temperature, rain, and sunshine, for example. How long a stem grows also depends on where it develops, and how many other branches there are. Only some of the lateral buds develop into branches, but there are so many that if they all grew to their fullest possible extent, they would be much too crowded. They would shade each other, and there would not be room for all of them. Many branches grow only an inch or even less each year. Some grow for one or two years and then drop off.

Branches need a certain amount of sunshine during the growing season, when they have leaves. If they do not get enough light, they die. For this reason, the lower branches often die after they have been shaded by upper branches for a few years. Eventually the dead branches fall off. When a tree is several years old, its trunk is usually bare for several feet above the ground.

The lower part of the trunk is the oldest part of the tree. Here the bark is filled with deep ridges and furrows, but on this tree the locations of the leaf scars and the scars of lost branches are still quite visible.

In future years, as the trunk becomes wider and the bark becomes thicker and more furrowed, the scars of leaves and fallen branches will become more difficult to see. It will, however, be many more years before all traces of them are gone.

scar of
fallen
branch

leaf scar

During its approximately twenty years of life, the trunk of this tree has been increasing in width. In the lower photograph it is shown at one-half its actual size. Above is a terminal bud, also one-half actual size. Although it may look dead in winter, in years to come a bud like this one may produce a trunk as large as this one or even larger.

Last autumn the winged fruits of the sugar maple tree turned brown and fell from the tree. Those that dropped on a windy day were blown away from the tree. Others — those that fell on calm days — fell directly under the tree or very near it. Of course, not all of them are still here. Squirrels have eaten some of them or carried them off, and fungi have rotted others away. But a few — whole or broken into their two halves, or even partially decayed — lie on the ground.

If you open a fruit, you will find a seed that looks much as it did in summer, except that now it is brown. At this time of year it is more difficult to peel the seed coat away, for it is dry and tough and clings to the embryo inside. But if you do succeed in removing the seed coat, you will find the embryo still green. Its cotyledons grew in length during the summer and are even more folded and crumpled than they were in early summer. The folding of the cotyledons makes very efficient use of space, for a large embryo now fits tightly inside a relatively small seed.

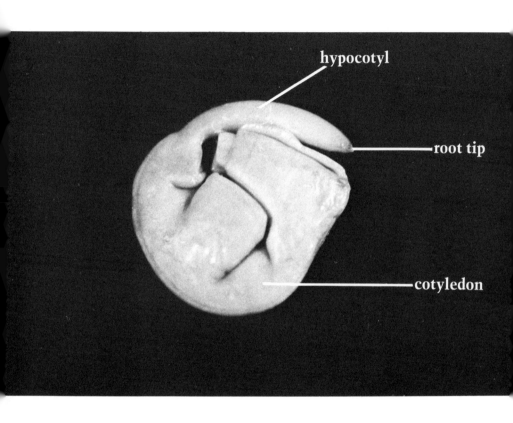

hypocotyl

root tip

cotyledon

The buds on the tree are not the only sugar maple buds that are surviving the winter. Each embryo still alive has a tiny bud between the cotyledons. You can see the bud if you spread the cotyledons apart. This is not easy, because when the cotyledons began to fold, they were pressed tight against each other, and they both folded the same way at the same time. Notice how well the two cotyledons would fit against each other if they were brought back together again. They look a little like pieces of a puzzle that were meant to make a perfect fit.

The bud between the cotyledons is very small. Here it is magnified 9 times. Yet this tiny bud is the beginning of the trunk and crown of a new maple tree.

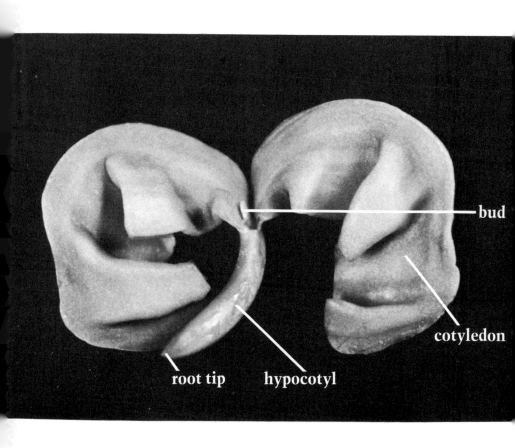

bud

cotyledon

root tip   hypocotyl